THE BOOK

JERKY BOYS

frank

HarperPerennial

A Division of HarperCollinsPublishers

First Edition THE JERKY BOYS: Johnny Brennan and Kamal. Cover and interior design: Roger Gorman/Reiner Design. Art: S. M. Taggart.
Contributing writers: Keith Blanchard, Bob Golden, Jack Mason, and Jed Spingarn
ISBN 0-06-095136-2
95 96 97 98 99 RRD 10 9 8 7 6 5 4 3 2 1

Hey, jerky!
That's right,
I'm talking to you,
rubberneck!

Welcome to **Jerkytown**
home of the tough guys,
wackos and fruitcakes.
It may not be much to look at,
but...it's home.

So, how did we wind up in the beautiful full-color coffee-table book ya got in your hands? It all started when those lunatics at the publishing company gotta hold of us. I'll tell ya, **I was pretty pissed off.** I was lying down to take a nap and the silly bastards were bothering me with the phone and their silly little book deals.

Anyhow, one of these suits hauls her ass over here, and she's all happy about stumbling on a gold mine. I told her to take a look around the joint. I grabbed her by the throat and dragged her up and down the building. She couldn't believe the shit she saw. **Sol in 2B**—hemorrhoids so bad you could take his pulse from his back pocket if you grabbed him just right. **Tarbash the Egyptian magician** with his fuckin' snakes and sabers. There's a **fucking wacko left over from World War II** who keeps some kind of **Mexican workboy** in the basement—don't ask. And you want fruit-cakes? Check out **Jack Tors in his penthouse.** This guy's got a small collection of shit up his ass. Yeah, his place is really wild. Sweet little guy. So now I say to the broad, "Let's talk cash. Let's talk selling books!"

So I choked a wonderful deal outta her and with a good shoe to the ass, she was out the door and on her way back to her silly little office.

And here we are. Anyway, I think it's a cute, funny little fresh kind of thing. I really hope you enjoy the book there, nibbles. I'm very prouda ya!

Rizzo

10

A tough guy who doesn't let you get a word in edgewise and tells *you* what's up.

pico

26

An Egyptian suffering from 1,001 Arabian nightmares.

TARBASH

meet the

Sol

64

A nervous, frail little man with an anxiety for every occasion.

Kissel

40

The neighborhood's old-timer who longs for the good ol' days—before the pinkos took over.

54

A boy from the barrios who'll do anything to stay in the U.S.—even work for Kissel or pick daisies.

79

A flamboyant hairdresser who is always in the know. He *is* vogue!

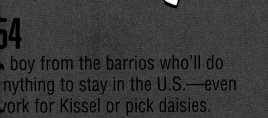

Jack Tors gang

C'mon, toughguy, you want a piece of me? You wanna throw down, punk? Okay, show me what you got. That's right, step inside so's I can show you what it's like to choke on your own nuts.

Frank's Favorite Movie Scenes

The In-Laws (1979): The scene where that fruitcake Peter Falk is tellin' that Shelly to **run around and "serpentine."** Man, that's crazy as a motherfucker. I make my wife do that when she's gettin' me a can a' beer or some eats. **But now, get me my dinner!!**

Scarface (1983): The scene where the coke dealers **chop off Al Pacino's partner's arms with a chainsaw**. Rrr-rr-rrr! Rrr-rr-rrr! That poor bastard! He's fuckin' screamin, there's blood sprayin' everywhere—**now that's a fuckin' movie.**

Commando (1985): The scene on the plane, where Arnold Schwarzenegger grabs the terrorist that's supposed to be watching him, he grabs him by the head and twists it and breaks his fuckin' neck. Then he tells the waitress, **"Hey, bitch; don't wake my friend**, he's dead tired, you fuckin' bitch." Dead tired! **Fuckin' classic!**

Dirty Harry (1971): The part where Clint Eastwood goes **ballistic and starts kicking the crap out of everybody.** Actually, that's pretty much the whole fuckin' movie. All those sorry-ass sizzle-dicks better look out! **Make my day, you fuckin' bastards!**

Steel Magnolias (1990): The part where Sally Field finally **breaks down and cries** at her daughter's funeral. I never laughed so hard in my life. **Now that's what I call comedy!**

So You Wanna Buy A Used Car...Or What?

(Transcript from official police report.)

Time:14:45 pm Central station

Officer Harry Johnson: Please state your name.

Frank Rizzo: I'm Frank. Frank Rizzo. You got nothin' on me.

Johnson: Mr. Rizzo, what were you doing on the lot at Pagnucci Bros. Used Cars yesterday?

Rizzo: I was selling fuckin' cars. What the fuck do you think I was doin'?

Johnson: But Joe Pagnucci claims he never hired you.

Rizzo: He's a fuckin' lying bastard. I talked to him on the phone.

Johnson: But he says he never actually hired you.

Rizzo: I talked to him on the fuckin' phone. I told him I was comin' down the next day to start work.

Johnson: When you went to the lot, why didn't you go to the office to speak with him?

Rizzo: Because, there were customers I hadda deal with. When I work, I work, fruitcake.

Johnson: The Berkowitzes—that's who you're talking about, right?

Rizzo: Yeah, the fuckin' lowlife Berkowitzes.

Johnson: And what happened with Mr. and Mrs. Berkowitz?

Rizzo: They was lookin' at a '83 Honda Civic and I says, "You wanna buy this fuckin' car, or what?"

Johnson: And is this your usual sales strategy?

Rizzo: You laugh, but it works. It works real good.

Johnson: What happened then?

Rizzo: Well, she gets this shocked look on her face, like she never seen a salesman grab his crotch before. And he says, "Excuse me?" Just like that, like he's the fuckin' king of the world.

Johnson: They were shocked at your language?

Rizzo: No, they spoke English. Open your ears, jackass! I never said they didn't speak English.

Johnson: And then what happened?

Rizzo: (mocking) And then what happened? And then what happened? I bashed his fuckin' head into the windshield, that's what happened. He was givin' me the evil eye, and I grabbed him by the back of the head and smashed his face like a grapefruit into the fuckin' hood of the car.

Johnson: I guess I should remind you again of your right to have an attorney present during questioning.

Rizzo: Fuck that shit. All I need's a bloodsucking lawyer in here tryin' to fuck me in the ass.

Johnson: Okay. So anyway...

Rizzo: So then she screams, and I say, "You're kind of a looker; you wanna hop into the back-seat with me and take this thing for a test drive?" I'm good like that, with the ladies.

Johnson: And what did she do?

Rizzo: So she runs off, completely hysterical. Fuckin' lunatic broad.

Johnson: And what about Mr. Berkowitz?

Rizzo: Him? (Laughs.) He just sort of laid there, all spread out on the hood. His face was pretty beat to shit. Looked like an old piece of brisket. Looked pretty funny to me, if you wanna know the truth.

Frank Rizzo's
Hangover
Companion

Unplug the phone and don't let no one talk too loud. Lose the wife and kids, or you're just gonna have to get off the couch to pop 'em when they start yabberin'. If some jackass outside starts layin' on the horn, take a fuckin' baseball bat out there and bash his lights in for him. You don't need that crap.

Forget about goin' to work. You're just gonna get fired for gettin' pissed off and breaking some fruitcake's head for looking at you funny, or choking your supervisor for getting on your ass about puking all over his shoes or some shit.

Nothin' takes your mind off the pounding in your head like watchin' some other fuckin' clown gettin his ass pasted. Turn the tube on and try and find the Three Stooges, or Bugs Bunny, or some Ninja movie with a lotta Chinese guys kickin' the crap out of each other.

Eat a bunch of burgers if you can. I slap down six, eight, twenty burgers, if I'm really fuckin' knocked out from drinkin'. Just sit on the crapper and chow down on big greasy burgers wit' cheese and try to shit my liver out!

Aspirin don't do nothin' by itself— you gotta wash it down with at least a pint of Jack before it starts working at all.

Antonio's Pizzeria

Frank:

I can't hire you again, Frankie; I just can't do it. Not again. And just 'cause you married my sister, don't give me that shit about blood is thicker than water: I've given you more chances than you deserve, and I just can't take one more. Last time you came down here, you put two of my guys in the hospital. The cops said when they got there, you were standin' on Joey's neck, bashing Michael's head into the cash register, screaming something about turning his face into a pizza. What the fuck's that? I don't care how they was lookin' at you, Frankie, you just can't pull that shit. That was $1,200 in medical bills, out of my pocket, plus I had to replace the picture window. You know I love ya, Frankie, but it's time to get some fuckin' decaf.

Your brother-in-law, Antonio

Silver Spoon Charm School

Dear Mr. Rizzo,

Thank you for the rather exuberant interest you expressed in the vacant substitute teacher position at the Silver Spoon Charm School. Unfortunately, in light of your curious phone call of 11/17, the principal has advised me that we have no positions available for a gentleman of your particular... eccentricities. However, should we discover a need either to "put someone's face through a chalkboard" or to "smack some heads together and knock some fuckin' sense into them little bastards," you may rest assured you'll be the first applicant called.

Sincerely, Mrs. Joan Pigglebotham
Faculty Supervisor

This is Billy's Place. It's *always* happy hour here. American beer's 90 cents a glass, fag beer a buck fifty. Lotsa guys, a couple of broads—best fuckin' place on God's green Earth.
The music's pretty good: a lot of fifties crap, some shitkicker stuff, a couple of mick folk songs. The shit gets turned off when the game starts—and you bet your ass the broads cry a river over *that* shit, too.
This here's Hooch the Pooch. Cute, right? Go on, pet him. He'll tear you a new asshole. He guards the place. You hear him growlin,' you better hope to God you got a baseball bat on you or somethin'.

Rizzo's place

Here's where the action is: the bar. One time this fuckin' whore walked up, put her hand right on my pud—swear to God!—and said, "Lookin' for some company?" Fuck _me_! I didn't know whether to nail her right there or grab my wallet with both hands.

This is what happens to you if you got something cute to say about Billy's wife. Billy don't take no shit, you know what I mean.

Spewer's Profile:
Frank Rizzo
Occupation: Freelance asbestos
removal engineer

Most Recent Accomplishment:
Completed 32 hours of community
service in 12 hours by speeding a
schoolbus of senior citizens from
New York City to Epcot Center in
Florida at 95 m.p.h. all the way.

Last Video Rented: *Monsters of
the Gridiron*

Proudest Possession: Claw hammer
used by Frank Sr. to kill a scab
who crossed a picket line during
the 1938 strike at Smiley's
Doughnut Hut.

Last Book Read: *Talbott's
Encyclopedia of Tools, Vol. 6*
(Ratchet to Wingnut)

Quote: "I can size up a douchebag
the second I meet one. Something
deep in my pissack makes me
want to kick his freakin' head in
even before he opens his fuckin'
trap. I guess you could say I'm a
sensitive guy."

Drink: Fuck Spewer's. Drink JD
on the rocks.

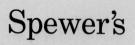
Spewer's

To the editor of Nuts & Bolts Magazine.

Listen here, you fruitcakes. You gotta get rid of that dipshit that does that fuckin' column testing cars for you guys. My head feels like it's gonna blow right off, I'm so fuckin' mad. That guy don't know nothin,' for Chrissakes. Ain't none o' you pinhead writers can get your pencil outta your ass long enough to drive a fuckin' car in the first place anyway. Who the fuck did this guy have to blow to get that job? I oughta come down there and break his fuckin' head. I'll tie his fuckin tongue to the back bumper of my 1978 Plymouth Duster and take him for a test drive. That's what I oughtta do.

You get me in there testin' cars for you, tough guy, I'll show you. Eighteen years I been testin cars. I got a toolbox, driver's license, all that shit. You don't have nobody down there knows more about cars than me. Race cars, stock cars, even fuckin' matchboxes: I'm good with all that shit. I'll take em up to a hundred miles an hour, two hundred, whatever, pop wheelies, all that shit. I'm crazy that way. I ain't afraid of crashin' or nothing. Someone cuts me off I'll ride 'em right into the wall, smash their fuckin' heads into the windshield. Just gimme the keys, and watch my ass take off. I'll come down there and start tomorrow, maybe I'll kick some fuckin' ass or maybe I'll just choke a few people. Then...I'll test some cars—ya got me, punk?

—F. Rizzo

Rizzo's
Deluxe Champagne Wedding

If you gotta be stuck at a god-damn wedding, the least you can do is get wasted off your crock on the free hooch. Here's what to do with the fuckin' champagne.

Ingredients:
2 oz. champagne in fluted glass
Small handful strawberries
8 oz. bourbon with ice

Directions: When everyone picks up their glasses for the toast, pour the champagne into your mouth without swallowing it. Turn to the little numbnuts silly ass waiter pickin' up plates next to you and spit it right into his fuckin' face. Start whackin' the bourbon down...and if you get a chance, give the groom a swift kick to the nuts.

Happy honeymoon, sucker!

* **Remember:** The more expensive a beer is the more of a dumb-ass sucker you are for lettin' them fuckers rip you off for it.

* **Don't drink none of that shit from other countries,** especially if we beat them in World War II. No schnapps, no saki—stick with scotch, tequila, and good old American Irish whiskey.

The Frank Rizzo
Drinking Guide

* The four best friends a guy could have are Jack Daniels, **Johnny** Walker, **Jim** Beam and J...

* Don't drink nothin' with fruit or straws or umbrellas or any of that crap, neither. **That shit's strictly for pussies.**

* Don't drink and drive. If some jackass bastard cuts you off, you don't want a lap full of Jack Daniels.

* **Wine is for broads.** Capiche?

* **Always have an extra beer open,** even if you're drinking something else. You don't wanna sit there like an idiot empty-handed while you're waiting for your fuckin' wife or the bartender to get you another drink.

k

Cuervo.

Hello?
Hello?

Roofing. How ya doing? Listen…all right…look…I gotta little problem here. I got some leaks up in the roof there. I had some guys here yesterday, some Mexicans…little Mexicans…up there wackin' away at my roof. They tell me this, that and the other thing. Next thing ya know it rains, I got the rain coming right down inside…I went up there…ya know they try to show me this, that…I fired the two of the fuckers off on their fuckin' head. They don't know what the fuck they're doing up there! My wife's up there pokin' around. She's makin' like she knows what the fuck is up…
I fired her down onto the fuckin' car.

Hey, now what I need here, buddy, is I need this fuckin' thing done right. Tell me what you can do for me.

No, I'm not fuckin' puttin' you on, man. This is aggravatin' me now. This shit's goin' on along…my wife she's up there like she knows what the fuck she's doin'. I kick her right up the fuckin' ass, threw her down onto the fuckin' car.

Show me what you can do now. I…I…really need this…it's all along the side of the fuckin' house. The water's coming in like a sieve.

Hey…this is a fuckin' joke, huh? Come on, buddy, help me out here.

Frank Rizzo. R I Z Z O.

Yeah now, this problem, this has been goin' on for years now. Ya know what I'm sayin'? The rain just comes in, it's like buckets on my fuckin' head. It's gettin' outta line now. I got the fuckin' kids up there playin' on the fuckin' roof. This is bullshit.

All right, listen. What do ya do? Ya go up there with the kettles, the pots, the fuckin' hot shit…what do ya do…talk to me.

All right 'cause ya know what happens here…I gotta lot of fuckin' problems. These little…these little Mexican fuckers, they were up there with the hot shit…and they're fuckin' jokin'…they were up there slapping each other with the hot mops. See I don't need this kind of shit. All right. So I hadda go up there—I threw the two fuckers right down in the yard. Split their fuckin' heads…outta here.

I don't know the name of the fuckers. I thought I was gonna get a little break on the price. The little bastards are up on the roof, runnin' around like fuckin' retards. One of 'em come through the fuckin' winda…he thinks he's cute…he's playin' his little games. He fired his friend through my fuckin' winda…he landed down in the livin' room. Hey…I can't have this shit.

All right, Bob. You help me out there. All right. I want you to come over here, you look at the fuckin' roof. You get your hands right in there and get your hands fuckin' dirty and you see what the problem is. All right, we'll see if we can fix this shit up. OK. All right, if I get in your way, or anything like that, you fire me down into the fuckin' yard…OK?

All right. Bye.

HIGH SCHOOL HIGHLIGHTS

Hyman R. Kapland High School

SOLOMON ROSENBERG

J.V. Hygiene Club; Young Jewelers Society; Pres., Roy Cohn Fan Club

"Hey Solly, nice nosebleed!"

Voted: "Best Shoes"

Known for: suing Shop teacher after burning tongue in kiln

Most Likely To: collect disability

"My bowels are on fire!"

"Goat-herd" understudy in *Fiddler on the Roof*

"I'll sue you into your grave, you bastard!"
—Dad

Fiorello LaGuardia Vocational School for Wayward Boys

FRANK RIZZO

Varsity wrestling (record: 12 and 0, 1 death); Pres., Future Spot-Welders of America

4 assault trials, no convictions

Most Likely To: head the AFL-CIO

"I'm good like that, dude!"

Voted: "Best Mob Ties"

Youngest driver in state to have license revoked

Known for: vast tool collection

"If I ever become a heroin addict with a leathery face, bash me bloody head in, he? There's a good lad."
—Keith Richards, 1964

High School for the Performing Arts

JOHN TORS

J.V. Soccer (masseur); H.S.P.A. Light Opera Club (sole member); Candy-striper

"Who stole my hand lotion!?"

Most Likely To: grow a handlebar mustache

Headed strike for salad bar in cafeteria

Voted: "Best Hair & Nails Advice"

Known for: fainting in bio class

Trini in "A Chorus Line"

Last Seen: having a late supper with drama teacher Mr. Peaslee

"Music and laughter were all they were after at the Copa..."
—Peter Allen

St. Margarita's

PICO

2nd conga, mariachi band; State Junior Champion, Green Bean Picking Nationals

"But I swear my green card's in my other pancho!"

Voted: "Best Night Vision"

Most Likely To: make less than minimum wage

Owned car insurance for half a day in 1989

"My name is El Pancho, I live on a rancho, I earn my five dollars a day. I go to my Lucy, she give me some poocy, and take my five dollars away."
—Traditional

KISSEL
(first name unrecorded)

J.V. Boxing; oldest 11th-grader in N.Y. State history (age 24); youngest bartender in N.Y. State history (age 12); Vice-Pres., Future Building Supers of America

"Where's my uncle Freddy?"

Puked on Pres. Roosevelt during speech to parents in '32 campaign

Voted: "Best Neck Girth"

Most Likely To: serve his country and get rid of the commie bastards!

"What a funny coincidence!"
—Lou Gehrig, on being told he had Lou Gehrig's Disease

Most Exalted High School of the Nile

HALI "THE SVENGALI" BALI TARBASH

Mgr., Varsity snake-taming team; Pres., Little Pharaohs Magic Club

"Give to me back my lunch money, you stupid...!"

Most Likely To: enjoy congress with the hindquarters of a camel

Voted: "Best 'Tight Turban' jokes"

Lowest pain threshhold in Mr. Khali's torture class

"*(ηιερογλψπηιχσ ηερε)*"
—Ramses III

Come quick, call police! Mr. Rizzo just burst into my home and took my monkey Babu. Now he is beating him with a ratchet! Stop hurting my little friend. I curse you. Aahh! Oohh! Help me, please!

LIFE LESSONS FROM THE FRONT SEAT OF A CAB

VERY FIRST DAY DRIVING. I drive taxi, I am picking up Japanese couple. They want to go to LaGuardia airport. I am most happy to bring them there. But on the way, sonofbitch truck nearly sideswipes me, I smash head on dashboard. I am dizzy, we get lost. Finally at airport, meter is $97. Japanese tip me $20, all smiles.
LESSON: I LIKE JAPANESE VERY MUCH.

VERY SECOND DAY DRIVING. Stuck in Midtown Tunnel, must urinate something terrible. Bumper-to-bumper going nowhere. Must make water extremely emergency. Loins quivering to point of bursting. Bite my lower lip so hard starts bleeding. On brink of very bad self-mortification.
LESSON: ALWAYS CARRY EMPTY SOFT DRINK CONTAINER. (ACCURACY COMES WITH PRACTICE.)

LAST WEEK THE WORST THING YET: Sitting at red light in bad neighborhood. Man opens passenger door, gets in next to me. Points big gun at my belly. Wants all my money. I tell him I just got on, only have $17. He punches me in the mouth. Says try again. I give him my wad of singles, about $50. He smiles, says he knows the singles trick. Says will shoot me now. Pulls trigger. Flag pops out of gun saying Bang! He grabs me, kisses me on lips, and runs away.
LESSON: KEEP MOUTHWASH IN CAR

AFTER ONE MONTH DRIVING. First experience with unruly drunk. He comes out of Blarney Stone in Wall St. area. Abuses me verbally on trip uptown. Falls asleep, can't wake him. Flag down police—they get address from his wallet, as well as my fare plus five dollar tip for my troubles.
LESSON: RICH DRUNKS ARE PEOPLE, TOO.

ECOND UNRULY DRUNK. Different story, a few months later. Big biker man, ry evil smelling. Calls me every bad name he knows. Camel fucker. Sand easel. Says my mother must have had relations with a giant toad. I stop, ll him very angry "get-out- of-my-fucking-cab." I open his door, try to rll him out. He pulls me in by the nose. He chokes me. He is laughing while am turning blue. Ancestors be praised, as I am fading into unconscious, y hand finds umbrella under seat. I jab and jab him until I am free. ESSON: TALK SOFTLY (TO LARGE LEATHERY FELLOWS) AND CARRY A OINTY STICK.

END OF ONE YEAR. I hit my first person. It is old lady, just brush her when making turn. She falls, she's yelling like warthog stuck with saber during magic act. I jump out to help her. She whacks me with cane, breaking my nose. She hits me so hard on the shinbones. She scratch me like mountain cat. Crowd has to drag her off me. LESSON: BEWARE OF ANGRY GRANNIES.

TARBASH TIME LINE

1780 BC Aarba the Younger
Zoser, Ruler of Egypt, returns his magic mummy box, claiming trick did not work and refusing to pay. Aarba receives punishment of "1,000 Cuts."

1950 BC Sarbah the Elder
Sestoris I invades Canaan but at home Sarbah, the king's magician, is hung by his tongue for desecrating sacred burial ground.

1570 BC Basha I
At dedication ceremony of Temple of Karnish, Basha makes fatal error performing "Crocodile Disappearing" act.

1460 BC Basha II
During sideshow at Feast of Luxor, Basha II attempts to levitate hippo; unfortunately loses concentration and is crushed like raw egg.

1361 BC SaAli
Accidentally killed during Tutankhamen birthday ceremony when exploding obelisk trick backfires.

1304 BC Basha III
Ramses the Great offers prize for best magic trick. Basha wins honorable mention with Jackal-in-Turban act. Makes insulting remark and is executed by Ramses himself.

EGYPTIAN HEXES, VEXES, CURSES, AND ASPERSIONS FOR ALL OCCASIONS

ASPERSIONS TO CAST UPON NON-TIPPING TAXI CUSTOMER:

MAY YOU DRAG ALONG STRING WHEN YOU PLAY WITH THAT THING.

MAY 1,000 BEETLES ENTER YOUR PILE HOLE.

MAY YOUR WIFE SUDDENLY GET LOST IN THE STREETS OF MOROCCO, THEN TURN UP AT MY UNCLE HALI'S HAREM FOR SALE AT COST.

MAY YOUR SON'S ONLY FRIEND BE A DONKEY IN HEAT.

TARBASH'S ALL-PURPOSE BLESSINGS AND BLASTS

MAKE YOUR FAMILY CONTENT BUT MAKE YOUR COBRA REALLY HAPPY.

KEEP THE GOAT FOR MILKING NOT FOR WOOING.

PLAY WITH A CAT EXPECT A SCRATCH. PLAY WITH A DOG EXPECT A FLEA. PLAY WITH A CAMEL EXPECT NEVER TO MARRY.

A WOMAN IS ONLY A WOMAN BUT HALVAH, NOW THAT'S A TREAT.

GIVE A HUNGRY MAN ONE FIG AND YOU TEACH HIM NOTHING. BUT SHOW A HUNGRY MAN HOW TO GROW FIGS, AND HE WILL CHARGE YOU THREE FOR A DOLLAR.

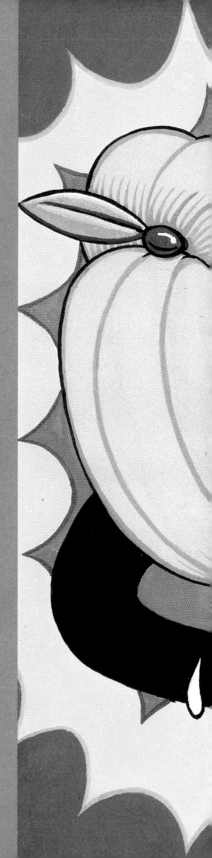

TARBASH TIME LINE

1250 BC Tabar

Kicked out of Pharaoh's palace for tasteless joke about sun god Re, Tabar takes revenge by informing Moses when the Red Sea will be at its lowest tide.

1188 BC Tikabash the Warrior

In attempt to rectify Basha I's failure, Tikabash performs the "Crocodile Disappearing" act with even less success than his ancestor.

332 BC Taghbar

Historian Herodotus visits Egypt and writes, "I witnessed one of the local fakirs, Taghbar by name, hiccup while placing a scimitar down his throat. I have never heard such screaming."

30 BC Sarnebhet the Midget

First ancestral mutation, Sarnebhet the midget grows up being ridiculed for his size. To compensate, he makes wisecrack to Cleopatra's handmaiden. Four days later he is fed to Bengal tiger in opening ceremonies at Coliseum.

130 AD Abdul the Wise

Emperor Hadrian founds new capital at Antinopolis and bans all magic from the city. Abdul (a.k.a. Basha XXXVIII) assumes writ does not apply to Romans. As ibis pecks out his eye as punishment, he discovers it does.

Tarbash Medical Woes

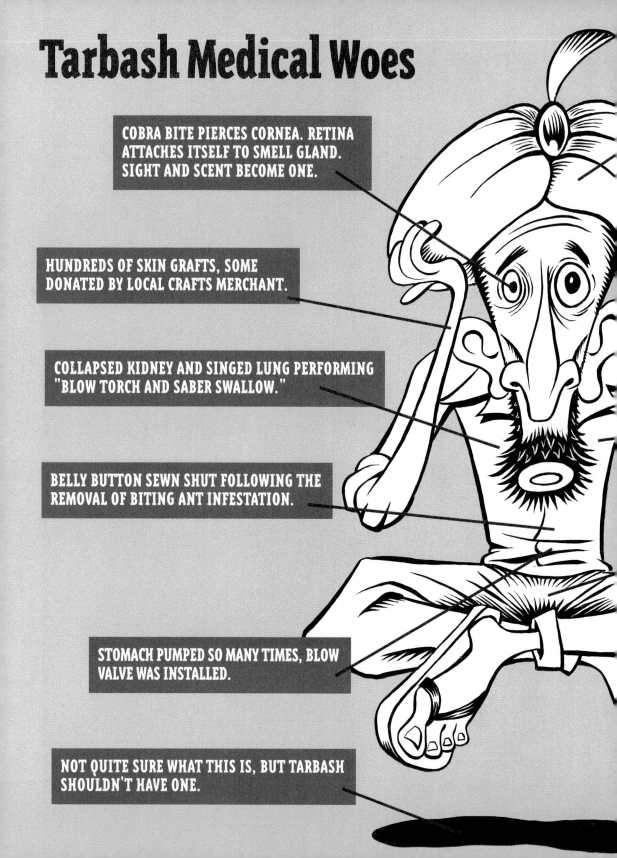

METAL PLATE INSTALLED FOLLOWING BIKE ACCIDENT WHERE TURBAN GOT CAUGHT IN SPOKES.

HAND SEVERED AND RE-ATTACHED MORE THAN ONCE...SUCH IS A MAGICIAN'S LIFE...

MIRACULOUS RECOVERY AFTER SPINAL COLUMN IS SNAPPED BY CRAZED MANGABEY.

PULMONARY ARTERY AND VENTRICLES REPLACED WHEN ONLY CERTAIN ORGANS VANISHED IN "DISAPPEARANCE TRICK."

ORIGINAL GENITALIA STILL INTACT ALTHOUGH PROSTATE THE SIZE OF SMALL THIRD WORLD COUNTRY.

PATELLA SPLATTERED WHILE SINGING "HAPPY & PEPPY & BURSTING WITH LOVE."

PROSTHETIC FOOT. ORIGINAL WAS LOST DURING STINT AS PIANO MOVER.

TARBASH TIME LINE

1217 AD Bashabat the Gimp
The fifth crusade against Egypt fails. Bashabat tries to perform "Four Horses Pull the Magician" feat. Due to bum leg, Bashabat trips and is drawn and eighted.

1316 AD John of Tarbash
The search for the mystical Prester Ontar leads to Ethiopia. The pilgrims are entertained by the magic of John of Tarbash. John is whipping audience into frenzy when he foolishly attempts fatal family "Crocodile Disappearing" act. Show comes to an end.

1618 AD Trashbash the Egyptian
Europeans discover the lost city of Timbuktu and are entertained by the slight-of-hand of Trashbash, an Egyptian exile. He follows them the length of the Congo when they fail to pay his bill.

1799 AD Tabar the Idiot
Napoleon conquers Egypt. Tabar is kicked to death for attempting to offer the short Corsican a slab of stone from a quarry outside Rosetta which he claimed had magical writings that would unravel the mysterious hieroglyphs.

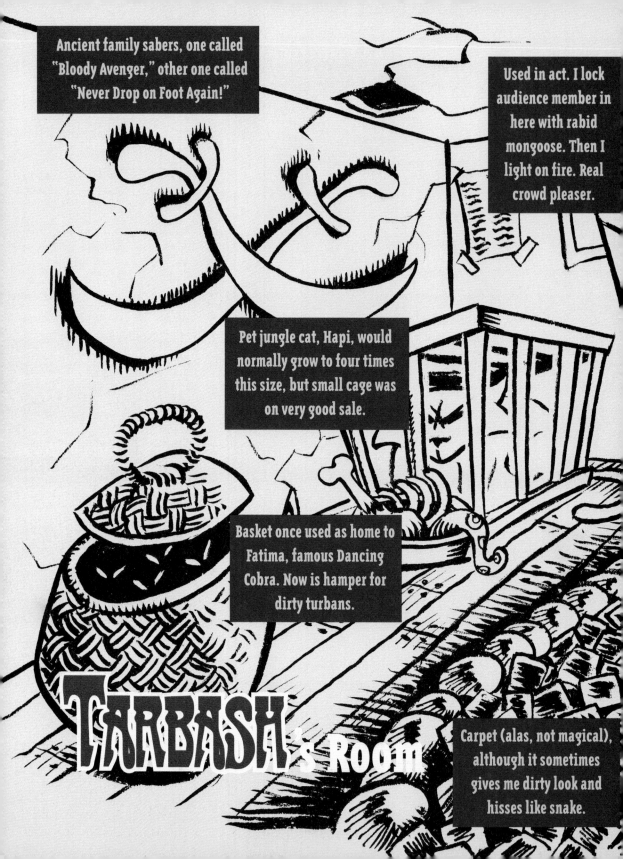

Dangerous animal trick been passed down from generation to generation. There are three principles in Tarbash Family Credo. Learn from me and you have no problem with animal.

CREDO

1. ANIMAL HAS MIND OF HIS OWN...EXPECT MISHAP.
2. NEVER LET AUDIENCE SEE YOUR PAIN.
3. ANIMAL WHO MESS UP TRICK MUST BE FIRED.

APPLICATION OF CREDO
(WITH EMERGENCY TIPS AND FIRST AID)

TRICK: "MONKEY IN THE MUMMY SUIT"
MISHAP: MONKEY CHOKES MAGICIAN

Monkeys usually, by nature, friendly and cooperative. But not Babu, the sooty mangabey, whom I trusted as a son and who betrayed me! I perform trick with Babu at religious coming-of-age ceremony in Brooklyn. I dress him in mummy straitjacket and then place him into Egyptian burial box. Just as I close door, bubble gum from 13-year-old boy goes pop! Babu kick out coffin top. He bite at me...aaaaah! Then he grab my neck with both hands and tail...aaaaaaah! Tarbash find himself in mangabey choke hold.

SOLUTION: MANGABEY TESTICLE ORBIT RIDE

Appear calm. Make Babu attack part of act. Join screeching primate by enlarging lower jaw and opening mouth. Just before airway completely cut off, reach with both hands for Babu testicles. Crush primate scrotal sac. As mangabey ascend skyward, bow to audience, catch breath, and emit high-pitched scream. When Babu hit floor, use him like soccer football at penalty kick time. Exit Babu.

LESSON: NEVER TRUST MANGABEY!

TRICK: "CANTALOUPE-FALCON-EXECUTIONER'S HATCHET JUGGLE"
MISHAP: FALCON FLY THE COOP

Falcons are professional and reliable. Not Baruch—Arabian bird I work with for years before he betray me. I perform simple street juggle with deadly executioner hatchet, melon, and Baruch. First few tosses fine...then falcon decide to migrate. Tarbash take bite out of hatchet instead of ripe melon...aahhhhhh! Tarbash lower lip end up on street curb.

SOLUTION: RECONNECT BODY PART

Appear calm. Smile and bow to applause. When audience gone, take lip, wash carefully, and place unattached body part to nub where once was lower lip. Hold firmly for several days.

LESSON: BARUCH RETURN SEVERAL WEEKS LATER AND MAKE EXCELLENT MEAL.

TARBASH DAILY REMINDER

Monday, February 6

Morning ritual: Pray for bountiful week, cleanse body, and recalculate net worth. Do laundry and repair favorite turban.

Throw away old goat milk, chisel and paint inside of refrigerator.

Ask tenants, "who keeps leaving case of potpourri in front of my door?"

1:30 PM: Appointment with Dr. Spargel (make sure to ask him if stool in urine is bad thing).

When driving cab in afternoon, figure out big finish for "Disappearing Chest" trick.

8:30 PM: Romantic candlelit dinner date with Serena (bring Bob's Big Boy coupon for free salad bar) ..also, feed (and this time chain) jackals before leaving apartment.

If not lucky with Serena, come home and put wig and makeup on Babu, then close my eyes and pretend.

NEWSCLIPS

BROOKLYN LEDGER MARCH 18

Man Wins Unusual Lawsuit Against Post Office

Manhattan, N.Y., March 17 (Reuters) A federal jury awarded $5,000 in a civil court case today to a man who sued the U.S. Postal Service for mental pain and physical suffering caused by late mail and abusive postal employees. Sol Rosenberg, 51, of Williamsburg, said of the court's decision: "These people were very rude and inconsiderate. They've made me an even more insecure person. I went to complain about my mail being lost or late. They spit on me, kicked me, and called me 'fatty-ass.' I don't know if I'll ever get over the humiliation. But the money helps."

MIDDLETOWN NEWS OCT. 24

Upstate Car Salesman's Hardsell Backfires

Middletown, N.Y., Oct. 23 (UPI) A salesman with an apparently well-known explosive temper was charged with aggravated assault after he attacked a customer in the Circle Hyundai showroom on Route 9. Frank Rizzo, 45, repeatedly rammed James McHugh's head against a car's fender after the 25-year-old Albany resident hesitated on closing a deal to buy a car from Rizzo. McHugh, who suffered cuts and bruises, was treated and released from the hospital later that day. He told reporters, "That guy's a certified menace. All I said was that I wanted to think it over."

QUEENS GAZETTE JUNE 12

Magic Show Goes Haywire

Queens, N.Y., June 11 (AP) A goat used by "Tarbash the Egyptian Magician" in a performance at Far Rockaway Junior High went on a rampage after being lit on fire by its owner. The magician, a 31-year-old Bangladeshi native living in the Williamsburg section of Brooklyn, said that his goat has been set on fire for years without incident, but that lately "Basra been acting very strangely and not eating well. I'm concerned he may have a tumor. I love that damn goat." After being doused with kerosene, the six-year-old goat charged into the audience and trampled several adolescents watching the show. The magician was arrested and charged with reckless endangerment of minors. The goat was treated for a singed coat and released from St. Joe's Veterinary Clinic later that day.

BROOKLYN LEDGER MAY 25

Husband Secures Restraining Order Against 300-lb. Wife

Brooklyn, N.Y., Aug. 20 (AP) A 70-year-old Williamsburg man received court protection against his overweight wife in a family court ruling today. Kissel [no first name available] alleged that his wife was terrorizing and physically abusing him with hand tools from his used hardware shop. "She would come after me with a sledgehammer, a crowbar, anything she could get her hands on to hurt me with," said Kissel. In court papers filed by Mrs. Mildred Kissel, she claimed that she was "just trying to motivate the lazy, stupid bastard to get out of his easychair and get a life. So I tried to pound some sense into him now and then? Since when is that a crime?"

THE STAR JAN. 12

Man Hospitalized After "Kooky" New Year's Eve Party

Manhattan, N.Y., Jan. 1 (CONUS) A member of a group of New Year's revelers was taken to St. Vincent's Hospital early this morning where a Persian melon was removed from his rectum. According to police reports, Jack Tors, 31, of Williamsburg and several friends began launching melons with skeet-shooting equipment after ringing in the new year. The melon-flinging took place at a boisterous party in a West Village brownstone. Said a friend of Tors, "Things got a little kooky after midnight. Everyone was naked and crazy drunk. I think Jack even fired the first melon and things got out of hand after that."

QUEENS GAZETTE SEPT. 6

Undocumented Immigrant Uninjured In Boiler Explosion

Brooklyn, N.Y., Sept. 5 (AP) A 21-year-old illegal Mexican was fortunate to escape injury after a boiler he was cleaning blew up. The blast sent the man, known to neighbors only as Pico, straight out a window and 150 feet into the air onto the roof of an adjacent building. The building's supervisor, Frank Rizzo, said of the incident, "That little grease-ball's got more lives than a damn cat."

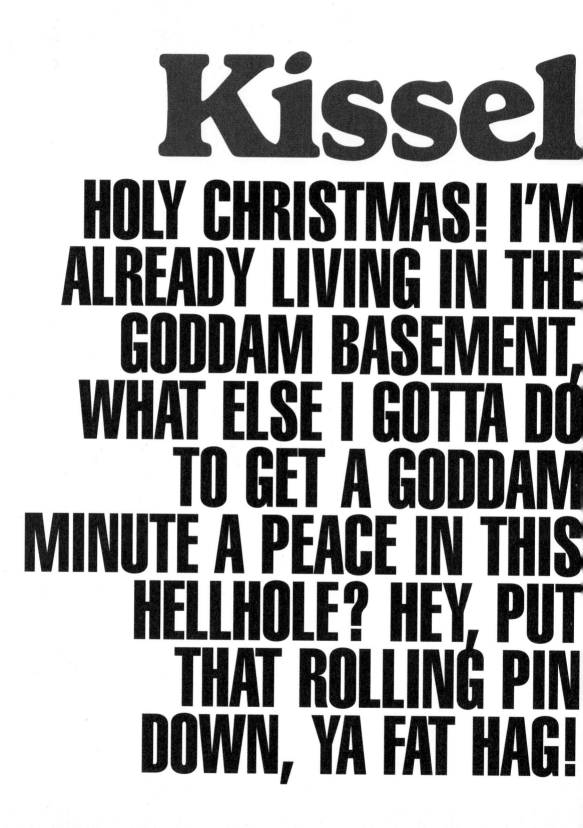

Kissel

HOLY CHRISTMAS! I'M ALREADY LIVING IN THE GODDAM BASEMENT, WHAT ELSE I GOTTA DO TO GET A GODDAM MINUTE A PEACE IN THIS HELLHOLE? HEY, PUT THAT ROLLING PIN DOWN, YA FAT HAG!

A "then and now" rambling of things that were better in the old days.

Then: Neighborhoods were nice, quiet and peaceful .
Now: All the foreigners took over and started to stink up the joint. I can't even play pinochle on the stoop no more.

Then: We knew who our enemies were.
Now: I can't tell the difference. They all look alike. Maybe we should drop a capsule of mustard gas on all of 'em.

Then: Boys liked girls, and girls liked boys.
Now: Girls gotta wee-wee and guys gotta fee-fee. How the hell do they tell each other apart?...Where the hell's that newsboy—they gotta sale at the department store—I need a new pair of spats.

Why the World's Goin' to He[ll] in a Handbasket

Yap, Yap, Ya[p]

Then: Women knew their place.
Now: Women gotta act like men all the time, wearing pants, goin' after guys' jobs. I swear to God, none of 'em even knows how to cook or sew.

Then: A family could make it with just one salary and eat meat every Sunday.
Now: If you have meat more than once a week, it's probably that "scrapple" stuff, which ain't really like the good stuff.

it's disgusting

DISPATCHES

The Magazine of the Greater Brooklyn-Queens V.F.W.

Volume 42, Issue 8, August 1992

"OLD SOLDIERS"

An Oral History, Part Four of a Series
Corporal Kissel (ret.)
"YOU JUST KEEP ON FIGHTING"
(Recorded and transcribed by Brett Weir)

In 1945, Kissel was a skinny 20-year-old kid from Brooklyn nicknamed "Kissel the Missile" by his fellow GIs for the remarkable speed and the accuracy with which he unerringly hit the mess tent. After serving in a reserve battalion that mopped up behind General George Patton's valiant march to Berlin in '44, The Missile landed back stateside. The next year he met a neighborhood girl named Harriet Adler, who persuaded him to marry her by pretending to be pregnant. The Kissels settled down in Williamsburg and opened a hardware shop. Today they only sell used tools and snipe at each other mercilessly. Over the decades, Kissel has become an ornery, kvetching fellow, but a patriot to the core. This is his story.

"When I was discharged in '45 I came back to a country that knew what the hell it was—the goddamn leader of the goddamn free world. People knew their place. They knew right from wrong. This was a helluva town and the Dodgers were some kind of ball club.

"I say give me the Old World Order any day. At least you knew who was on your dance card. We took care of them Nazis, and when we were finished kicking the krauts' asses, we had a bunch of commie bastards step right into the bad guy role. Life was good. A dollar bought you something in those days.

"Now who the hell do we have to fight with? A bunch of camel jockeys who'd just as soon blow themselves to take one freedom-loving white man along for the ride?! What about them dipshits up there in North Korea? Think they can make an A-bomb with their puny little graphite reactors? You got the goods?! Show me, you little yellow hillbillies!!!

"You ask me, we shoulda taken care of that whole situation back when we had the bastards up against the Yalu River in '51. Just like we shoulda done the job right in Southeast Asia, fighting there like a pack of girls on a camping trip—evacuating every one of those brownie bakers by whirlybird every time somebody got nicked with a piece of shrapnel. 'Send me home, Sarge, I cut myself shaving my legs.'

"Hell, I got more metal in me from my goddamn hip replacement last year than those Desert Storm bleeding Purple Hearts with their bumps and bruises.

"I guess you could say some of us veterans of the Big One are a might upset about this gutless trend that seems to be devouring the U.S. of A. We're pissed. And you know what? If time healed all wounds, none of us would have belly buttons!!!"

USELESS CRAP MY DAMN WIFE BOUGHT ON TV

Some kinda little vacuum that sucks up your hair and cuts it off. Never used.
The battle-ax gave it to that freak Jack Tors upstairs.

A contraption to squeeze juice outta food. Stupid idiot doesn't realize
I need more roughage, not less.

A set of crappy videos that tell Bible stories in cartoon form. Criminy,
we don't even have one of those tape machines!

The Time-Life Library of Indian Cooking. Like I would eat that crap? Threw
the damn set out, but I think Tarbash picked it outta the garbage.

A thick rubber suit that was supposed to help her sweat off a few dozen pounds. Ha!

A whole closetful of crap for her damn cats: coats, booties, playpens, and "gourmet"
treats. What ever happened to makin' 'em find their own damn mice?

A damn lamp made outta a giant seashell.

A pack of giant rubber bands that you're suppose to pull and tug on for
exercise. Yeah, pull this, ya fat old warthog.

A bunch of painted plates with pictures of the Great Depression. Used
them for a little skeet practice. Very good for *my* depression.

4 September 1994
General Colon Powell (Retired)
Department of the Army
Pentagon Building
Washington, DC, USA
Reference: Tech Sgt. Kissel (#US 45782312-Retired)

Dear General:

First of all, I gotta say that back in WW 2, I had nothing to do with keeping you coloreds from the front line fighting where I was most of the war—and up to my neck in filthy dirt and taking orders from a dumb Polack lieutenant who didn't know you know what from shinola. No, I always says, "Them colored boys deserves the same chance to take a direct hit from a mortar shell or a slug in the belly from a kraut bullet."

I write because I gotta complain to a Republican someone about what asshole Clinton is doing messing up the Army with fairies and dames. I mean who wants to be in a foxhole with some limp-wristed faggola painting Day-Glo sparklers on his entrenching tool and singing, "Dance with me, Henry"? Not Kissel. I'm an American.

Let's talk about showering. With a platoon filled with them la-di-da nancy boys, what American soldier is gonna stride bare-assed into the john without worrying about taking some daisy boy's schlong up the backside like Pearl Harbor? Not Kissel. I ain't no prevert.

Women in the service! First of all you and I both know a jill what enlists in Uncle Sam's Army is a lesbo-butch-dyke looking for love in all the right places. O.K., so even if a couple of these bitch warriors are straight, what's a red–bloodied guy gonna do if he's inside a tight-quartered Sherman tank with some broad what smells like a stale flounder because she's having the monthly curse? Not Kissel.

You got to run for President in 1996 and get rid of this cluck from Arkansaw. You got my vote and the vote of all the other Kissels.

Yours in the front line,

Tech Sgt. Kissel

Kissel's to-do list

Sweep cig butts and little tiny red-capped bottles off front walk.
Fix busted light in the back room.
Clean that goddamned toilet.

This week no dinner until it's done right.

Climb up on roof and fix TV antenna.

This time, put a mattress on the street first in case you fall again.

Tell that towelhead magician to turn down that goddamned music.

*Pico, tell that idiot I'll get the super to smash his fingers in the door
again if he doesn't shut it up.*

Fix my dinner.

Easy on the hot stuff!

Pop zit I can't reach on lower tush area.

Maybe he could scrape my feet, too.

Climb down the sewer grate in front of the house and get that quarter I dropped yesterday.
Look into getting hairpiece.
Polish and clean all guns.

Stay away from the ammo or I'll have Immigration all over your skinny little ass!

Immigration & Naturalization Service
Employment Confirmation Form
(This form, to be completed by applicant's employer, certifies that the
applicant for citizenship is gainfully employed in the United States at the present time.)

Name of employee:
Pico

Position:
He's my little Mexican guy.

Company or Firm:
Kissel's Used Hardware.

What are employee's responsibilities?
Running around like a goddamn monkey breaking things and stealing from me,
bothering the wife, scaring customers, etc.

How long has employee been on your payroll?
Seems like since the beginning of the goddamn universe.

How many hours in the week does the employee work, on average?
Same as me. Every goddamn day from 5:30 a.m. to dinner, then it's time for
his odd jobs (give me my bath, massage the wife's feet, etc.).

What is employee's rate of pay?
Three hots and a cot, plus whatever peanuts and daisies the little bastard
can steal and send back to Mexico, or wherever the hell he's from.

Has the employee received any tips, bonuses, or additional monies?
Gave him a pair of pants that didn't fit me anymore. He uses one of the legs
as a sleeping bag.

Does the employee receive any health benefits?
Yeah, I don't use my full strength when I give him his beatin'! That benefits his health, you bet!

How would you rate the employee's job performance?
Better than doing it myself.

**Do you know of any reasons your employee should not be allowed to pursue
citizenship?**
Yeah, he's a goddamn Mexican! How's about we all just move to Mexico and
give them the whole friggin' country?

Additional comments:
Yeah, $5 is missing from the register! You tell that little wetback I'm
lookin' for him!

Date: Jan. 26, 1995

Employer's signature: _____

PICO-BOO!
How I Keep the Fear of God (and Me) in the Little Brown Bastard

Nearly saw through broom handle, then tell him to sweep up the shop.

Slip laxative into his burrito.

When giving him orders, say things like "Don't forget to clean out the spanglenook," or "Pick up my bandersnatch at the cleaners."

Get him to try on my old Boy Scout uniform and then send him up to that freak Jack Tors with a bouquet of forget-me-nots.

Have him give the Old Bag a pedicure.

Make him watch my Mt. Rushmore vacation slides.

Send him over to the boys in the 43rd Precinct with a note pinned to his chest that reads, "I am a Cuban terrorist. I have a stick of dynamite up my pendejo. You cops are a bunch of maricons with badges."

Slip catnip into his overalls, then send him down to feed the alley strays.

Make sure he gets "special" fortune cookie that says: Do whatever boss tell you, or your cajones will fall off.

Have Hilda from Excellent Escorts dress up as a trooper and wake him from a dead sleep at three in the morning.

Lend him videotape collection of "Cops" episodes.

Get a Vietnamese kid to come by and offer to work for $25 less a week.

Rent a robe and gold wings and hire Rizzo to play the Angel of Death come to take poor Pico away. Save his sorry ass and win his eternal gratitude.

pico

mariposa! I no can come up to fix your pipe right now. meester kissel say I
must clean his guns and then spit polish the kitchen floor or he say he
give me a boot in the pinga.

Pico's Points of Entry

Pico evaluates various methods for entering the U.S. from Mexico.

Method 1: *Disguising yourself as a border agent and walking through customs backwards.*

Thees one sound easy, but they mus have I.D. cards, or sometheeng, cuz nobody got fooled at all when I tried it, man.

Method 2: *Digging a tunnel under the fence.*

Eet's too hard, man! It takes you forever!

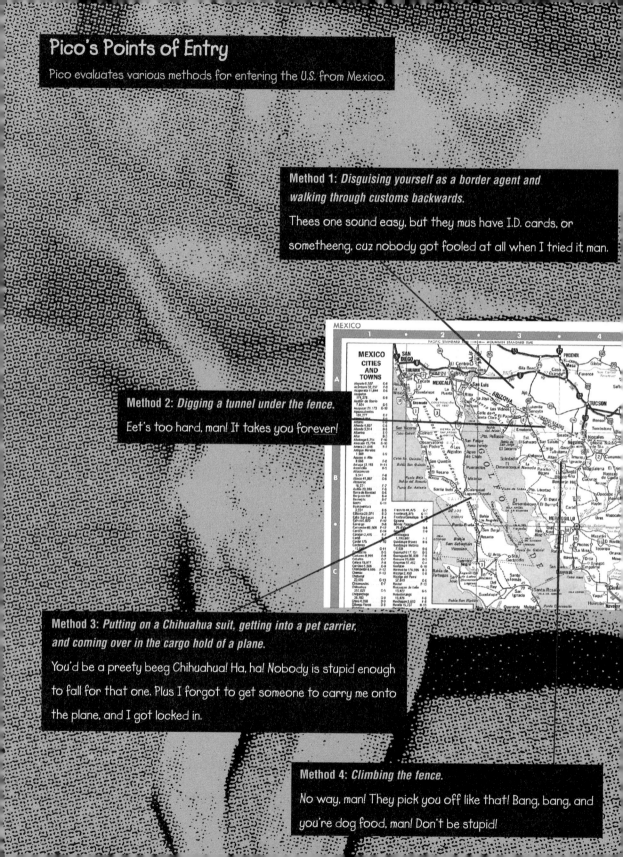

Method 3: *Putting on a Chihuahua suit, getting into a pet carrier, and coming over in the cargo hold of a plane.*

You'd be a preety beeg Chihuahua! Ha, ha! Nobody is stupid enough to fall for that one. Plus I forgot to get someone to carry me onto the plane, and I got locked in.

Method 4: *Climbing the fence.*

No way, man! They pick you off like that! Bang, bang, and you're dog food, man! Don't be stupid!

Method 5: *Climbing the fence, in a suit of armor.*

Well, they won't peeck you off, but eets so heavy! How you going to run away when you land on the American side? You can take off the suit so you run faster—but then they just peeck you off! You get what the problem is?

Method 6: *Climbing the fence, in a suit of armor, with a fast horse saddled up and waiting for you on the other side.*

Oh, man; now you just screwing around with me.

Method 7: *Stealing a passport from a tourist.*

It takes too long to find someone who looks like you. I tried this and <u>nobody</u> believed I was Elissa Goldberg, man. One of the guards did ask me for my number, though.

Method 8: *Applying for immigration papers from the Immigration and Naturalization Service and waiting your turn to immigrate legally.*

Yeah, sure. Bye, amigo! See you in six hondred years!

That's for suckers, man.

America on $5.00 by Pico

America is big place! And cost so much!
You no have much money? Here is Pico's ideas
for you to have good time in America for not
so much money:

Breakfast: Go into kitchen of rich yankee American restaurant and shout "Inmigración!" very loud until workers have much fear and leave. First, eat the food when they run off. Then take their jobs as dishwasher and eat expensive gringos' food! Quit job when full.

Lunch: Steal Taco Bell hat from sister, cousin, etc. Show up at Taco Bell and go right to kitchen. When boss is near, complain of fever and cough salsa onto food. Soon you and food are thrown in dumpster! Don't forget salsa!

Dinner: Go to crowded Chinese restaurant at dinnertime and say, "I am back! Where is next delivery?" Chinese give you big bag of steaming food for Jewish gringos to eat at home. You eat!

Hooker: Go to "chick with dick." Make with her the sex for $5.00! Already it is time to go home and go to bed after full day in America!

Don' worry, the ceiling's not falling down. It's just heavy from the hardware store upstairs. That crack, she's no' getting any bigger but I keep watching, just in case.

Now I lay me down to sleep.
I hope for night to pass.
I say my prayers with all my might,
So rats won't eat my ass.

They call this a futon, but it's like a bed, just no springs or head-board or nothing—just one big lumpy mattress. Kind of looks like a giant burrito to me.

CITIZENSHIP QUIZ

NAME: Pico Mariposa
NUMBER: 05539872

A. HISTORY

1. The United States won its independence from what country?
Panama

2. Who is referred to as "The Father of our Country"?
Sid Fernandez

3. Name two reasons why the Civil War was fought.
1) Low on tacos
2) Some guy turned hees dogs loose on crowd and everybody started fighting.
I don't know, theese was crazee.

4. "Prohibition" effectively halted what in the United States?
The sale of hot sauce because they would feed eet to the dogs, make them fight like crazee—and everybody would kick them in the cajones.

5. American laws and rights were the basis of what United States document?
The NAFTA

B. GEOGRAPHY

6. Name the two oceans that border the United States?
What would I know? I come from the fuckeeng desert? All I know is cactus!

7. Where is New Orleans?
Mr. Kissel sell it at the hardware store—it's good on brass, but it doesn't work good on wax floors. Believe me, I know. Sometimes I drink eet.

8. Which is the "Windy City"?
In my pants—we make the chili like bullets. My ass will show you some wind.

9. Where is the "White House" located?
In the U.S., gringo.

C. CULTURE

10. What sport is known as the "nation's pastime"?
Chihuahua fighting. Each man ties a Chihuahua to his back and they roll around in the ring until the Chihuahuas are crushed to death or bite each other silly—one or the other. The man slap each other too. It's funny to watch.

11. What animal represents the national symbol?
Chihuahua missing one eye. This shows he has heart.

12. Why is the holiday of "Thanksgiving" celebrated?
To get a hot meal and stuff your belly.

13. Who bombed Pearl Harbor and when?
I don't know, but Mr. Kissel, he say he was there and was bombed.

14. Name a celebrated American author and one of his/her works.
Sid Fernandez, How to Really Swing a Bat (Like a Stick at a Piñata)

Pico's Pico de Gallo Recipe

**You Will Need: One pair
of pants
with big pockets**

Directions: Steal two carrots anna cucumber from the ol' lady's garden next door. She'll never miss it, man.
Wait 'til the dog's asleep, though, or he could be like a peet bull, man, and you could get half your butt bit
off. Then get a big papaya from the fruit stand. If you don't got the money, just yell "Inmigración!" and
then when everyone runs, drop the papaya into your pants, and maybe a couple o' tomatoes por tu
madre. Then, get a can of pineapple chunks from the store and you're all set. Hide de can under your arm,
though, not in your pants: You don' want that puppy smackin' into your cojones when you
sneak past the cash register.
Then take down a bottle of Old Man Kissel's rum and mark it on the side with your thumb where the level is.
Pour in a bunch of the rum an' then go over to the sink and fill it back up to the level with water. He'll never
know the difference. But don't pees in it, no matter how funny you think it is, because he'll know for sure,
man. Jes' chop all those veg'tables up together and eat em up. Don' let him catch you in
his rum, though, or he'll kill you dead!

Sol

COULD MY APARTMENT BE GETTING SMALLER WHEN I'M OUT? IS THAT POSSIBLE? OH MY ASSY WARTS ARE KILLING ME! WHERE DID I PUT MY GLASSES? PLEASE HELP ME. OH, I'M FEELING DIZZY NOW. DO I LOOK FEVERISH TO YOU?

9 A M
10
11
12
1 P M
2
3
4
5

7:15 a.m.—The weather has turned for the worse, a bleak and rainy start to another intolerable week. I've had the dream about the fire engines again.

8:00—Oh God! Blood in my stool. The nurse in Dr. Witherspoon's office doesn't believe me and refuses to give me an appointment.

8:45—Anxiety over the BM crisis aggravates my shingles. I rub my back bloody in a doorway before finding my emergency supply of cortisone. My hands shaking, I fill a syringe and start jabbing my back like a pincushion.

11:00—Very distressing mail. Some kind of mix-up with the prostate results, have to take all the tests over again. Notice from IRS about last year's return. Subscription to Model Railroader has expired.

12:00 p.m.—Scour the Help Wanteds, call two ads—offer a brief summary of my skills and experience. When the subject of my salary requirements comes up, both calls are mysteriously disconnected. Follow-up calls prove fruitless.

2:00—Take a fitful nap. Wake up in a sour-smelling puddle. Oh, the heartbreak of bladder-control problems.

5:30—Jack pops in to try out a new idea for my hair. When he's done, my head looks like a zebra's ass that's been attacked by a pack of hyenas.

7:30—While watching "A Current Affair" report on psychosurgery, Rizzo bursts in and withdraws several pints of blood through my nose which he explains will serve as payment for back rent.

9:30—Tarboosh's monkey escapes, climbs through a vent, and bites a chunk out of my calf. I manage to dislodge the monster by banging it against the radiator.

11:00—Sleep evades my weary heart as the Kissels downstairs get into another free-for-all. I really think someone is going to be killed down there.

SATURDAY, JULY 22

9 A M
10
11
12
1 P M
2
3
4
5

9:00 a.m.—Oh what a beautiful morning, oh what a beautiful day!! Slept like a baby. Woke to a sunny, low-pollen Saturday. Even the pigeons on the roof sound happy, happy, happy. Cherry blintzes for breakfast washed down with a piping pot of Darjeeling and my regular assortment of pills, vitamins, ointments, inhalers, and suppositories.

11:00—Jack Tors in 5B has me up to watch "Mighty Morphin Power Rangers" and "Animaniacs" (boingy, boingy, boingy!). Later we trim Jack's bonsai trees. Don'tcha just love a lazy weekend morning?!

1:00 p.m.—Mail arrives! Oh boy! The results from my prostate tests were all negative!! And the first payment from the Post Office lawsuit has finally shown up.

3:30—To celebrate my little windfall, I splurge on a few luxuries at Waldbaum's: a beautiful new set of tweezers, that new enema kit I've had my eye on, a digital thermometer (rectal), and one of those air ionizers to suck the dust and smoke from the air. Oh boy, lucky me!

6:00—Mr. Kissel sends his cute little errand boy Pico up to change the mousetraps. For an extra $10—hey, spend it when you got it, I always say—Pico agrees to give me a sponge bath. What a nice young man.

10:30—After a baked chicken (skinless) dinner from the corner deli, I fall asleep watching Abbott & Costello vs. Dracula on "American Movie Classics." What a day!

July						1995
S	M	T	W	T	F	S
						1
2	3	4	5	6	7	8
9	10	11	12	13	14	15
16	17	18	19	20	21	22
23/30	24/31	25	26	27	28	29

SUNDAY, JULY 23

5:30 a.m.—Awakened from a semi-sound sleep by screams...Jack and his friends from the city are having one of their predawn wrestling parties again.
8:45—Finally get up after tossing and turning for the rest of the morning. Burn the roof of my mouth sipping a cup of too-hot chocolate.
4:30—Get an erection while feeding the fish. (Must remember to ask Dr. Spencer about the meaning of this.)
8:00—The unbearable Frank Rizzo pounds on the door, demanding this and last month's rent. I pretend not to be home. Rizzo opens the door with his pass key and finds me hiding in the pantry. He chokes me silly and leaves bruises all over me.
10:30—Erection returns while brushing teeth. Mr. Peepers and I salvage a fleeting moment of glee from this otherwise forgettable Sunday.

A M

9

10

11

12

P. M.

1

2

3

4

5

MONDAY, JULY 24

SOL HAS A GOOD DAY, A SO-SO DAY AND A VERY BAD DAY

1995
W T F S
2 3 4 5
9 10 11 12
6 17 18 19
3 24 25 26
0 31

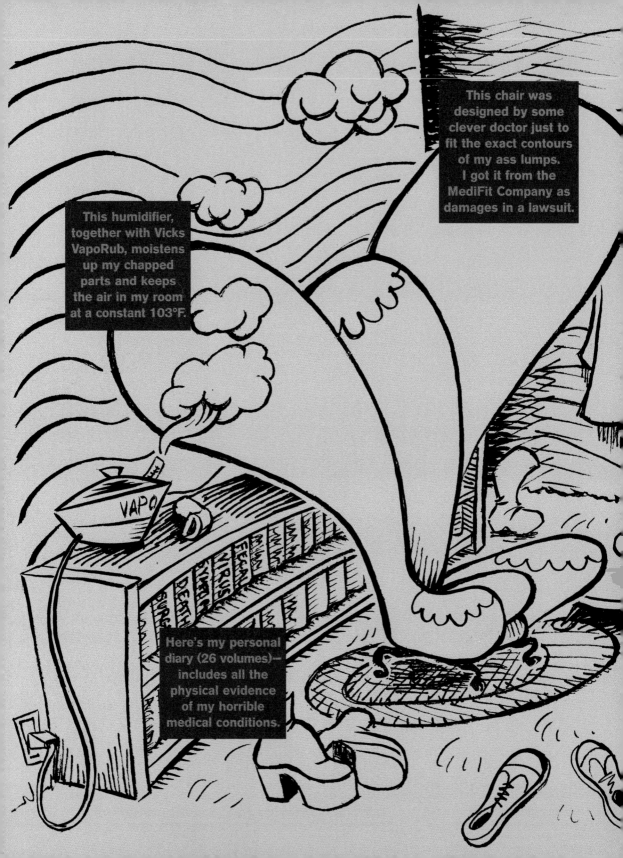

Sol Rosenberg
Emergency Room Records

FRONTAL

Eyes
—Weak; some retina damage due to poking by others.
—Emergency room visit on 12.2.89, complaining his "eyes is going crazy." (Regained composure after being slapped and given cocoa.)

Nose
—Near-total blockage of nasal passages; no evidence for patient's claim that he is "allergic to his brain."

Ear
—Minor hearing impairment due to massive, ancient wax deposits.

Mouth
—Admitted to E.R. 3.7.67 having swallowing tongue during anxiety attack. Patient claims attack brought on by neighbor's purchase of mountain cat for use in magic act.

Left Nipple
—Severe chafing. Cause unknown.

Stomach
—Severe gastrointestinal disorders characterized by overactive acid ducts, resulting in volcanic expulsions of purple, methane-rich gas and feces. Condition referred to as "Rosenberg's Syndrome" since1979.

Genitals
—Admitted to E.R. 9.12.88 complaining that his "freakin' genitals is burnin' up" due to an allergic reaction from eating asparagus. Patient later admits masturbating with Vicks VapoRub.
—Admitted 7.3.93 with scrotal sac caught in zipper. Patient fainted during sewing of two stitches.
—12.22.92. Patient is permanently barred from donating sperm in New York State due to low semen motility and chronic tendency to miss cup.

Toes
—Multitude of corns, bunions, and planter's warts.
—11% fungus coverage.

DORSAL (Ass)

—Massive scarring around anal pore incurred during childhood "fart-lighting contests" at camp, patient claims, though tissue samples indicate much more recent damage.
—Admitted to E.R. 1.3.82 with massive, inflamed boil on left buttock. Shock and blood loss incurred during lancing render patient critical for 3 days.
—Ingrown hair in anal cavity compounds with hemorrhoid to render both inoperable. Toxic shock places patient back on critical list 3.3.90.
—6.7.93. Patient complains agitatedly of a "flamin' hemorrhoid inside my ass cheek" and is refused emergency admission. Highly improbable condition verified 24 hours later as patient is admitted to O.R. in unconscious state.
—Laser surgery for compound hemorrhoids goes horribly awry 2.8.87 as patient sits on laser, directing intensely concentrated radioactive light beam towards lower colon. Patient's feces are rendered danger-ously radioactive for the remainder of his natural days, possessing a half-life of 2700 years.
—10.31.74. First appearance of anal warts.
—4.6.87. The start of what is to become the most prolific verifiable cases of anal warts on record and the only case in the literature of one anal wart growing atop a "feeder" wart. Patient sleeps standing up and complains of hallucinations.
—Patient rushes to emergency room in severe pain complaining that "my own shits is burnin' me up." Diarrhea sam-ples taken confirm acid levels in patient's feces possess pH level of 7.0, roughly the same as Drano crystals. (Shoulder)
—Mild bursitis

Transcript of 911 Call (9/24/89 11:21 P.M.)

Dispatcher:

911. What's the emergency?

Sol:

Yes, hello. I'm very terrified...

Dispatcher:

Would you like to report a crime?

Sol:

Yes, I'm very frightened, please. (PAUSE) Hello?

Dispatcher:

What's the problem, sir?

Sol:

Yes, I dreamed I was in a dark scary place and there were some bad men and they were very aggressive with me and wanted to dance.

Dispatcher:

Excuse me?

Sol:

Yes, thank you. Scary men in my dream, I'm saying.

Dispatcher:

Sir, is there a crime in progress?

Sol:

No, but it was very terrifying and I was wondering if someone could come over.

Dispatcher:

I'm sorry, sir. You can't call 911 to report a nightmare.

Sol:

But they wanted to dance with me in a sexual manner and possibly hurt and kick me. They were very fierce with me.

Dispatcher:

I can't dispatch any officers without a crime.

Sol:

Well, maybe some of you could come over and just hold me and comfort me and rub Vicks VapoRub on my chest.

Dispatcher:

I'm afraid we can't do that.

Sol:

I'd make cocoa...

Dispatcher:

Sir—

Sol:

I pay taxes, goddammit!

(Dispatcher hangs up.)

J. MERKLE SPENCER, M.D.
Psychiatrist
96 Fifth Avenue
Suite 10A
New York, NY 10011

Patient Name: Sol H. Rosenberg
Session #: 187
Date: June 17, 1994
Transcribed by:

DR. SPENCER: And how are we feeling this week, Mr. Rosenberg?

MR. ROSENBERG: Oh...not so good, Doctor. I think I'm getting a rash all over my ass and down the back of my thighs. Also on the way over here I got sort of accosted by these two big, ugly biker-types, and see they really got me good. They were pinching me silly, I mean like real hard on my belly here and here and...and then they said they wanted to spank me with a spatula and make me crawl around like a dog and then—

DR. SPENCER: That's all very interesting, but—

MR. ROSENBERG: —so I curled up in a tight little ball like some kind of weird creature I seen on a nature program and I—

DR. SPENCER: Mr. Rosenberg, why don't we just pick up where we left off last week? [Sound of paper shuffling] Let's see...I believe when we ran out of time we were talking about your fear of...oh yes, here it is. Biscuits.

MR. ROSENBERG: No, no. I didn't say I was afraid. I was just making the point that I had no idea they even had biscuits in Italy. Italy, of course, I'm afraid of, because it's shaped like a boot, and boots have quite often been used to kick me up inside my ass very hard and whatnot.

DR. SPENCER: Are you sure there isn't something about biscuits that makes you uneasy?

MR. ROSENBERG: Say, does it smell funny to you in here? Like an old dog or a wet pillow with ointment on it?

DR. SPENCER: Mr. Rosenberg...you're blocking again. What did we learn to do about that when we were in our last session?

ROSENBERG & SPENCER: Relax...Focus...Breathe...Breathe...Breathe.

[A few moments of breathing interrupted by the sounds of choking and gasping]

DR. SPENCER: Mr. Rosenberg! Mr. Rosenberg! Are you all right?

MR. ROSENBERG: [Gasp]...I'm okay, I'm all right. I just suddenly remembered those awful men saying how if I didn't drop on all fours and play Poochie Boy for them they were gonna beat the balls off me. Said they would pile-drive my face into a fire hydrant until my nose started gushing blood. I'm telling you, Doctor, it gave me an awful fright and now I have a very strange feeling in my nose and throat, a real itchy-like, stuffed-up kind of—could you maybe prescribe for me some kind of expectorant, a cough-syrupy thing to help me get some of this phlegm up? It's terrible. I feel like a backed-up sinus basket! They said I was their little nipple boy, and that they would stomp on top of my assneck. I keep thinking that I'm chok-ing on my own—

[Sounds of violent coughing, gagging and spitting]

DR. SPENCER: Are you all right now, Mr. Rosenberg? Do you think we can continue?

MR. ROSENBERG: Oh yes, Doctor. Thank you for asking. I'm feeling much better now.

DR. SPENCER: Very well. Last week we began talking about your obsession with your father's genitals.

MR. ROSENBERG: Actually, I believe we were talking about the tattoos I put on my dog's nuts!

DR. SPENCER: I stand corrected.

J. MERKLE SPENCER, M.D.
Psychiatrist
96 Fifth Avenue
Suite 10A
New York, NY 10011

Treatment Case Summary

Patient, Sol R., is a 51-year-old unmarried male who has been in therapy for seven years. Lives alone in a Williamsburg tenement. Slightly overweight, acutely myopic. Does not exercise or bathe regularly. Is generally confused, anxious, and intermittently delusional. Experiences episodes of paralyzing fear countered by incidences of manic, polymorphous sexual fantasizing. Patient reports a variety of physical, psychological and psychosomatic ailments including: feelings of inadequacy, grandeur, superiority, or invincibility. Suffers from insomnia, narcolepsy, a persistent ringing in the ear (no neurological basis), and a strong dislike for the smell of raw celery. Allergic to squirrels, nutmeg, wax, roll-on deodorants, and MTV.

Only child, parents deceased. A sickly youth, the patient reports being bullied frequently. Schoolmates reportedly called him "Six-Eyes," "Pencil Pud," and "Bum for Brains."

Has been consistently ambiguous about his sexual orientation. Believes he may have been "warped" by a pre-adolescent experience with a second cousin (once removed) with whom he played various bathtub games he recalls as "Submarine Salvage" and "Lighthouse."

Complains frequently about beatings inflicted on him by the building supervisor, a Mr. Rizzo, and seems to be particularly interested in the behavior and activities of neighbor "Jack the Hairdresser."

PROGNOSIS:

While patient feels he has made significant progress in the last five years, it is difficult for his therapist to concur. True, patient no longer weeps uncontrollably during evening news, doesn't wet the bed nearly as often, and is taking a class in macrobiotic Hungarian cooking. But significant pathological processes remain. Patient lies, misremembers the simplest facts, and easily slips into a fantasy world. Have recommended doubling sessions to twice weekly, have consulted Dr. Garnisp about a preliminary evaluation for electroshock treatment, and have ordered a comparative battery of CAT scans.

Sol's Medical Corner

(Warning: The medical opinions expressed in this column do not reflect the views of the publisher. The publisher is not responsible for any pain, bleeding, or injury that may result from the advice contained below.)

Dear Sol:
I use sunblock, but I still freckle quite easily on the beach. Should I be using a stronger SPF?
Concerned

Dear Concerned:
You don't fool me! You people were very mean to me at the nude beach last week, including many who pointed at my parts and whispered and threw seaweed. It made me very angry! I'm never going back there again. I still have sand all up me, and little bitty coral shells.

Dear Sol:
I have a severe case of ass-warts. Also, my name is Alan Piles. Do you see the tragic irony?
A. Piles

Dear Alan:
No. Are you making fun of me? I was told everyone would treat me good. I hate this job. I think you people are very cruel.

Sol's Home Remedy #204:

Your ass is all chapped sometimes? Make an anal poultice using wonderful herbs all available from your local Korean grocery store.

1. Purchase1 box baking soda, 1 bottle tonic water, 1 block of tofu (soft curd) at Korean market.

2. Take home. Knead ingredients into clay with hands. Make it all warm, please.

3. Apply soothing clay on and about ass-neck. Pat briskly.

4. Chip off with screwdriver when hard. (DON'T STAB ASS!)

An icicle could fall off the roof and spear you in the throat.

Someone could slash you with a razor on the street for "dissing" him.

You could get tuberculosis from someone that has tuberculosis breathing on you.

Your hat could blow off at the beach into the ocean and you could go in after it and get stung to death by a jellyfish.

Things Worth Worrying About

There could be a horrible head-on collision and you could be standing in the crowd watching to see if any cars blow up and a mugger could take your wallet.

You could get a rash on your privates from the detergents they use at the laundromat.
There could be bacteria in your corned beef sandwich and you could start coughing up blood right there in the deli.
You might never have sex again.
You could twist an ankle getting out of a cab and fall and give yourself a nasty sprain.
You could get cancer from the radiation coming out of the microwave oven by the checkout stand at the 7-Eleven.
You could get leprosy from the toilet seat.
Someone could bump you on the subway and you could threaten to sue the guy for whiplash only to find out he's a hotshot lawyer who countersues you and takes all your money.
You could go to one of those peep shows and be looking at a naked girl and, you know, becoming aroused, and it could turn out to be your sister.

THE ROSENBERG
PHOBO-METER
Is Your Phobia Trivial, a Serious Concern or a Full-Blown Nightmare?

TYPE OF FEAR
TAKE A VALIUM
CONSULT YOUR FAMILY DOCTOR
GET YOUR ASS TO A LICENSED THERAPIST!!!

SPEAKING IN PUBLIC
Racing pulse, Watering eyes, Dry mouth, Blurry vision, Tongue bitten off during cerebral seizure

HEIGHTS
Can't look down from 5th-floor balcony, Get dizzy standing on a step ladder, Cannot stand up without tranquilizers

CLOSED SPACES (CLAUSTROPHOBIA)
Take stairs instead of elevator, Always leave bathroom door open, Prefer tumbling down a flight of stairs and having my shoes fall off

OPEN SPACES (AGORAPHOBIA)
Can't sleep outdoors, Eat in more than three times a week, Bedroom in closet and haven't left it since the '70s

WATER
Can't swim, Wouldn't take a cruise, Unable to swallow liquids

SEX
Uncomfortable with own body, Uncomfortable with anyone's body, Only comfortable watching the dog lick himself

PERSONALS

Frail Jewish man on disability with a cute muffin ass, 51, seeks companion for friendship or more. I enjoy long walks in my room, solid bowel movements, shoes. Oh boy, I have been mistreated in the past (kicked, poked with sticks, etc.), and I won't have that again. If you like Hebrew National meat logs and talk radio, and don't mind my painful ass disorders, this is your lucky day! Also, I might sue you. Thank you. Serious responses only. **Box #21432**

If you look out this window, you can see right into the Health and Fitness Club workout room. Work it, boys! Be careful, though——you can get a crick in your neck if you watch too long. Trust me on this one.

Can I whip you up an hors d'oeuvre? I make a fabulous grilled quiche puff. It's the yummiest thing you could possibly imagine. Present company excepted, of course.

Here's my lava lamp. Don't you just miss the seventies something fierce? I still have this white polyester shirt with great big pointy collars out to here in my closet. Play your cards right and you might even get to see it, sweetheart.

The Jack Tors Workout

Let's face it—nobody likes a custard ass, but with all the manimals at the corner spa these days, I'm lucky if I can pull myself away from the locker room long enough to hit the machines! Here's a crazy little regimen you can do at home to keep those niblets firm. Try it with a friend!

Stretching:

Many boys underestimate the value of limbering up. Big mistake! I dated a Romanian gymnast once who could actually kick himself silly about the head and neck, and let me tell you——that earned a big 10.0 from the American judge! My favorite little maneuver is the Monkey Jungle. Simply go into your bathroom and turn the shower on hot. Now both you and your friend take your things off and hang from the shower-curtain rod by your legs until you're all limbered up, just like two little monkeys in the rain forest, only these beasties can walk erect!

Bulking Up: Pecs

Ok, I admit it——there's nothing like a rack on a boy to make my nuggets do the cha-cha! Honest to God, my friend Peter could choke me silly and I wouldn't press charges because of his wonderfully firm bosom. But who needs all the grunting and sweating when there's a perfectly simple alternative? Simply fasten tiny barbells onto each nipple and go about your day until the pain and swelling are too intense to bear! The effect is temporary, so make sure you have time to hit the clubs later that night. I know one Hercules who'll be the belle of the ball!

Aerobics:

One very popular aerobic exercise in the gyms these days is boxing. Being punched and kicked by another boy is great for toning, or just for feeling wanted. If you are doing this one with a partner, it's important to remember not to hold back. One good way to begin is to accuse each other of being sluts and just start slapping. If you're like me, pretty soon you'll just be going fucking crazy—— pinching and spitting and really doing some damage. When it's over, have a good cry and towel each other off.

Bulking Up: Glutes

This is the big enchilada. Make those muffins dance and the world will come to you! Here's a firming-and-toning technique I learned in hairdresser camp which will really keep your dance card full. Simply oil up the pocket of your ass, place a softball in it and secure it with 7 strands of twine. Remove one strand of twine each day until, at the end of week, you should actually be able to hold the softball in place using the muscles of your ass! If you really work it, there's no reason you shouldn't one day be able to use your butt-cheeks to throw a grown man clear across the fucking room!

Quick tips 'n' hits

Stairmaster (Good for overall body condition)
Step One: Climb a flight of stairs.
Step Two: Throw yourself down them.

Clean and Jerk (Or is it the other way around?)
Step One: Honey, if you need help with this part, you've got more than an exercise problem.

Murphy Bed Press (Great for improving flexibility, but you'll need to make a friend to try it.)
Step One: Lay down on a hideaway bed or open convertible couch.
Step Two: Have a spotter or two fold up the bed or couch with you in it.
Step Three: Work out "I can't breathe" signal ahead of time. (Gee, maybe this should be Step One! Oops!)

Warm-Down

Back to the bathroom! Once again, turn the water on hot, but this time pretend you're in a Turkish steam room. A couple of games of "snap the towel" with your playful pasha, and you're ready to hit the showers.
Bon workout!

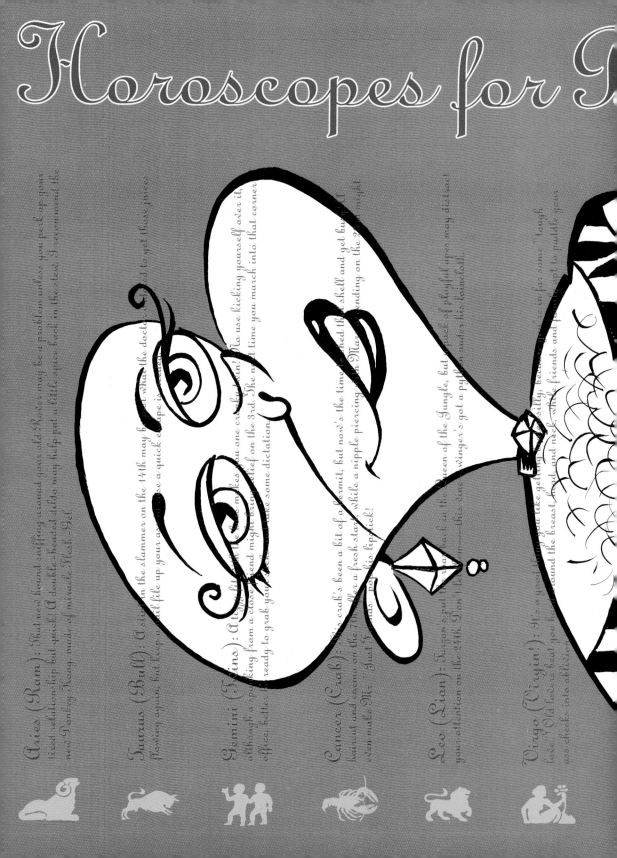

Aries (Ram): That new hound sniffing around your old Rover may be a problem unless you pick up your fixed relationship but quick! A double-headed dildo may help put a little spice back in the stew. I recommend the new Donkey Kong, made of miracle flesh.-Ied

Taurus (Bull): A slug in the slammer on the 14th may be just what the doctor ordered to get those juices flowing again, but keep a nail file up your ass in case a quick escape is in order.

Gemini (Twins): A twist of fate makes you one cranky bean! No use kicking yourself over it, although a spanking from a close friend might come in relief on the 3rd. She'll want time you march into that corner office, better be ready to grab your socks and take some dictation.

Cancer (Crab): This crab's been a bit of a hermit, but now's the time ... shed the shell and get busy! Offer a fresh start while a nipple piercing the Mars bending on the 23rd might haircut and enema on the 7th ... even make Mr. "Just Gonads" Bob his lipstick!

Leo (Lion): Sharqan's put the tiara back in the Queen of the Jungle, but a pack of playful apes may distract your attention on the 24th. Don't let 'em — this one winger's got a python under his loincloth.

Virgo (Virgin!): It's a good thing if you take getting so silly, because you're in for some "tough love." Old lovers that you knew around the breast, back and neck, while friends and family opt to paddle your ass cheeks into oblivion.

Libra (Scales): A couple of...

Scorpio (Scorpion): Scorpio gets a little...

Sagittarius (Archer): Nothing...

Capricorn (Goat): Brace...

Aquarius (Water carrier): She...

Pisces (Fishes):

Staten Island Stylist

The Borough's Leading Journal of Hair Design

Volume 3 August 1995 Number 8

Jack Tors: The Interview

Mid-Length Dazzlers

Sexy, Spirited Short Cuts

Jack Tors:
The Interview

Jonathan (Jack) Tors is a legend in the Island's close-knit hair community. A rebel, rule-breaker, trouble-maker, and bon vivant, Jackie Boy is one local boy who's made it very good in the world of hair. He attend-ed the High School for the Performing Arts (where he was active in theater and gymnastics, among other extracurricular activities!) and now works as a freelance hair designer and consultant for film and television, print advertising, fashion shows, private parties, and a long string of salons, most of them not gutsy enough to support his radical and avant-garde ideas about hair, beauty, and style. He currently lives in Brooklyn—"I've got an incredible space but my building is an absolute zoo"—but is a club-runner, occasional cross-dresser, and general boy-about-town also known in the demimonde as "Tors the Horse" for his well-known ability to "go the distance, even on a muddy track."

SI STYLIST caught up with JT at a very private party at The Markham.

Q: Jack, when did you first realize that you were a hair person?
JT: I think I always knew, somewhere inside. But it wasn't until I got my first bad cut that I fully understood who and what I was. I was seven and my mother Sylvia brought me to her regular salon—I think it was called "Gino's House of Beauty Magic" or something ridiculous like that—and that's where some brute named Dominic savaged me. My god I swear I looked like some kind of little freak boy toy by the time Dom was finished with me.

Q: Tell us a little about your teen-aged years.
JT: Oooh! holy shit, alright! It was like being in a holy you-know-what lunatic asylum, those years were. I was spending most of my time in the city, much of it in *Desperately Seeking Susan*–era gear, so much so that the guys on the ferry took to calling me the Material Boy. Well lemme tell you, snake hips, I showed a few of those sailorboys who was the captain and who was the first mate.

cntd. page 21

Jack demonstrates the "groove cut."

"Show me your torpedo and then you can sail it right into the bay."

"Ooohh. . . do you lift weights, sweetheart?"

Jack Tors

"Twist my nipples 'til they
turn black and fall off."

"What's a handsome guy like you doing with such a small nibbler?
What could you possibly do with that?"

"What's a nice guy like you doing
without my hands in your pants?"

"I wonder if you could possibly tell me why my furniture stinks so?"

"What's your sign? . . .
Mine's 'Slippery When Wet.'"

"Let's go to the gym and slap
each other silly."

"Would you like to guess what I could do
with a small bag of potatoes and
this funny little stick with a hook on it?"

Ten Pickup Lines

"Those are really nice cleats you're wearing—
but they'd look even better stuck in my ass. . . ooohh."

Jack's Tips and Tricks to Being a Good Roommate

Keep a list of your **phone sex calls** and I'll keep a list of mine so we don't have a problem at the end of the month.

Don't leave the lid off the **jumbo Vaseline jar** by the bed. All kinds of lint and stuff will get inside and we'll have to throw the whole thing out and it'll be a big waste.

Any **sex toys** you bring become property of the house for as long as you live here.

I get the bottom bunk. Period, case closed, end of discussion! I don't want to have to lay there on the top bunk all night with nothing to look at but the ceiling. Hello! Bing bong! My house. . . my rules!

"He who boileth the potatoes washeth the pot." Also, you're responsible for cleaning any stains on the wall from potatoes you fired. If you can't aim, don't play, **sweet balls!**

I don't care if you're woman, man, or goat: **it's rude to hang your pantyhose** over the shower curtain rod! It's the most annoying thing ever!

If your portion of the rent is late for whatever reason, you'll be subject to a penalty of my choosing, in whatever outfit I decide to dress you in. **No arguments, sailor!**

4. "PINECONE IN A BIG WAY"

3. "THE GROOVE CUT"

7. "PUMP IN CIRCUMSTANCE"

Jack Tors

2. "DUTCH WINDMILL"

4. "MR. 10½-INCH TOOLBOX"

5. "FIREMAN'S HOSE"

6. "FREAKY MR. GOODFELLOW"

8. "MR. HAPPY'S GOOD HAIR DAY"

9. "THE SOLICITOR GENERAL"

10. "RENALDO'S DAY OFF"

DETROIT LAWN MOW"

12. "CONTINENTAL EXHAUST PIPE"

13. "GARÇON TAKES THE DIRT ROAD"

14. "THE HAPPY TRINKET SWIRL"

Gallery of
Hair Designs

Jack Tors Styling Kit

Butt plug On a date, in a club or at that fancy costume ball—it's like having a tiny friend whispering in your ear all evening!

Utility knife An absolute <u>must</u> for the 90s stylist! Carve your initials into that special someone's head or slash your own face for a sexy pirate scar!

Anesthetic/syringes In the mood for a silly little kick-fight, but can't take the pain? Just butt-pop some Novocain and come out kicking!

Afro gel "Mr. Tyson is ready for his deep scalp massage now, Mr. Tors." Well, a girl can dream, can't she?

Kwik-Burn Kerosene A lighting fluid and fragrant body lotion for the fire bug in all of us. Nothing says love like a little 2nd degree burn!

Hog's grease Lubing up is sizzlin' fun when you add hog's grease to taste! "Sooo-ey!" (Now available in refreshing mint.)

Electric carver The hottest prop on

Vak-U-Blow 3000 Sometimes even a stiff penalty won't keep a hardened desperado down—that's when this cowboy just has to pack some heat!

Jack Tors Interior Decorating Tips

You can never have too many pillows. On your bed, on your divan, on your chairs: Pillows, pillows, pillows! They make you feel like a fabulous Arabian princess.

The last word on wingback chairs is no, no, <u>no</u>! Join your <u>decade</u>, sweetheart.

If you cook, like I do, make sure you have plenty of room in the kitchen, or you'll just make yourself <u>crazy</u>! You'll need room for accessories, too, like those cute cow oven mitts and an apron that says "Don't Bother The Cook: He's Positively Having A Panic Attack!"

No track lighting, except in your dance room or your cute little music room or whatever you want to call it, where you can have all kinds of silly little trinkets and lights flashing and whatnot.

Speaking of the music room, don't just put your CDs in the rack alphabetically, unless you're an <u>accountant</u> or something. Arrange them by <u>color</u>, so they cover the whole spectrum when you look at them in the rack and the colors make you feel so sexy. Now—isn't that better??

Every kitchen should have a cookie jar modeled after Quentin Crisp with the hairstyle and all. Just a personal preference.

Lacy curtains can be magical, but don't forget to put up some thick shades, too, just in case you don't want the neighbors to see just how good you really are—because they may not be ready to handle it!

Jack Tors

IF I WERE PRESIDENT

No more stuffy suits and ties. If I were President, everyone in Congress would have to wear lavender jumpsuits with fabulous silk scarves.

I'd call Boris Yeltsin every night on the red Moscow hotline phone and we'd talk just like a coupla best girlfriends about how our day went, and what was bothering us, and whether he thought I looked fat, all that stuff.

The White House would be transformed by a staff of sweaty airbrush painters into the Mauve-and-Fuschia-with-Almond-Accents House.

Since the Secret Service would have to watch my ass twenty-four hours a day anyway, I'd tell one of them to specifically watch my ass.

Cuba would have to wear a big purple cowboy hat at the United Nations as punishment until they agree to lose those drab army fatigues and bring back those little hot pants for fighting in that intense heat.

Instead of "The Star Spangled Banner," our national anthem would be "Where the Boys Are," as sung by Connie Francis, of course. And everyone would have to stand up straight.
For God's sake, it's only your country.

THE JERKY BOYS SPEAK FOR THEMSELVES

YOU GET ASKED THE SAME DUMB-ASS, OBVIOUS QUESTIONS OVER AND OVER. LET'S GET YOUR ANSWERS TO SOME OF THESE ROUTINE QUESTIONS SO WE CAN GET ON TO SOME SERIOUS PROBING…
Johnny Brennan: Go fuck yourself.

HOW DO YOU PREPARE TO MAKE A CALL—DO YOU MAP OUT AN IDEA FOR A GAG AND REHEARSE WITH EACH OTHER, OR DO YOU JUST FUCKIN' WING IT?
Kamal: We wing it, dude.
Johnny Brennan: Absolutely wung.

WHAT DO YOU THINK YOU'D BE DOING NOW IF THE JERKY BOYS HADN'T CAUGHT ON? WHAT WERE YOU DOING BEFORE THE JBS HIT?
Johnny Brennan: Testing mattresses at a mattress factory. (Right, Uncle Vinny?)

IF YOU HAD TO DONATE AN ORGAN—AND LET'S SAY FOR ARGUMENT'S SAKE YOU <u>HAD</u> TO—WHICH ONE WOULD YOU GIVE UP, AND HOW WOULD YOU LIKE IT TO BE REMOVED?
Johnny Brennan: My piss–sack and shanker. I'd have them removed with a good kick.

WHAT THE HELL IS AN "ASSNECK"?
Johnny Brennan: Look in the mirror, fucker!

WHEN AND HOW DID THE TWO OF YOU MEET?
Johnny Brennan: Long time ago, back in Queens, someone turned on the hydrant a few blocks up from my house and Kamal came floating down in this little basket and there was a little note pinned to him, telling me to hide him. It's really weird, but I had this sensation I had read about this somewhere before.

WHAT ARE THE ORIGINS OF SUCH CLASSIC RIZZOISMS AS "LIVERLIPS,"
"SIZZLECHEST," "FRUITCAKE," AND OF COURSE, THE IMMORTAL "JERKY"?

Johnny Brennan: When God put together my brain, I guess he, I don't know…dropped it?

WHO DOES WHICH VOICES?
Kamal: Well, Thunder is the voice of God.

WHAT ARE YOUR FAMILIES LIKE?
Johnny Brennan: We get together three times a week and eat shards of glass, play Johnny-Ride-the-Pony, and do cute little genital tricks.
Kamal: My parents are both bomb specialists working for the circus.

HOW DID YOU GROW UP?
Kamal: I was a drifter…

DO YOU POSSESS ANY ACTUAL EMPLOYABLE SKILLS?
Johnny Brennan: I don't boast about it much, but I have a Ph.D. in psychology with a specialty in human behavior.

HIT RECORDS, A MOVIE, NOW A BOOK—WHAT'S NEXT FOR YOU? AN EXERCISE VIDEO? A CALENDAR? A LINE OF CASUALWEAR?
Johnny Brennan: Actually, we're working on all that new stuff. Isn't that a coincidence, you jackass?

COULD THE J. BOYS GO INTERNATIONAL? PERHAPS "LES GARÇONS JERKÉ"?

Johnny Brennan: Why the hell would we do that? Picture Frank Rizzo headin' to France. As soon as the French heard about it, they'd be runnin' like chickenshit fucks to the high hills. I'd tear that Eiffel Tower down and stick it up some Frenchman's ass.

ON "SOL'S NUDE BEACH" YOU PRETTY MUCH FREAK OUT SOMEONE'S ELDERLY MOTHER. DO YOU EVER FEEL GUILTY FOR PERHAPS TRAUMATIZING A RECIPIENT?

Kamal: Never.

HAVE YOU GUYS BEEN APPROACHED BY THE SLIMJIM PEOPLE OR THE BEEF JERKY COUNCIL FOR POSSIBLE ENDORSEMENTS?

Johnny Brennan: Not till they make one just the right size.

DO YOU HAVE ANY MORE CONSTRUCTIVE HOBBIES?

Johnny Brennan: Yeah, I like to tie one on—go out into my fields and carry my cows from one spot and move them all the way over the hill to another spot. And then beat them down just for good measure. For some reason they seem to love this.

WHAT'S YOUR VISION OF HELL ON EARTH?

Kamal: A six-four-three doubleplay that kills a rally.
Johnny Brennan: Getting good 'n drunk and shittin' in the bed.

IF YOU HAD TO LIVE INSIDE A SITCOM, WHICH WOULD IT BE AND WHY?

Johnny Brennan: "The Addams Family," because I'd like to bang the ass off that little Pugsly kid.

DO YOU HAVE A FAVORITE BOOK?

Johnny Brennan: *The Prophet*.

FAVORITE MOVIE?

Johnny Brennan: *The Quiet Man*.

FAVORITE SONG?

Kamal: Theme from "Dolemite."

FAVORITE DRINK?

Johnny Brennan: Hair of the dog with a few shots of Jack.

FAVORITE MEAT PRODUCT?

Kamal: That's personal.

FAVORITE BRADY BUNCH MEMBER?

Johnny Brennan: They're all a pack of fuckin' idiots!

HOW MANY JERKY BOYS DOES IT TAKE TO SCREW IN A LIGHTBULB?

Johnny Brennan: Same as it does to stick it in your mouth and crush you like a piece of shit, you dumb fuck. What a stupid ass question.

AS WE APPROACH THE MILLENNIUM, WHAT'S YOUR VISION FOR THE 21ST CENTURY?

Kamal: A computer reading my lips through the pod bay door.
Johnny Brennan: My vision is that we as a people will all rise to our individual greatness and work together as one to fulfill our private dreams, separate and apart from others. And let no man put asunder...I ask you...what is the difference between an avocado and a mango? [Pause] Don't you see it's as simple as this. Because they both have pits. That is my vision, you fuckin' jackass!